# Concert and Contest COLLECTION

**Compiled and Edited by H. VOXMAN**

*for*

## E♭ ALTO SAXOPHONE with piano accompaniment

### CONTENTS

**RUBANK®**

**HAL•LEONARD® CORPORATION**

7777 W. BLUEMOUND RD. P.O. BOX 13819 MILWAUKEE, WI 53213

# At the Hearth
## (Au Foyer)
from Suite Miniature

A. GRETCHANINOFF, Op. 145, No. 8
Transcribed by H. Voxman

4

# Evening Waltz
### (Valse dans le Soir)
from Suite Miniature

A. GRETCHANINOFF, Op. 145, No. 10
Transcribed by H. Voxman

# Minuet
## from Haffner Music, K. 250

W. A. MOZART
Transcribed by H. Voxman

**TRIO**

# Mélodie

SIMON POULAIN
Edited by H. Voxman

# Canzonetta and Giga

LEROY OSTRANSKY

# Sonatina
### (Based On Trio V)

J. HAYDN
Transcribed by H. Voxman

# Andante and Allegro

ANDRÉ CHAILLEUX
Edited by H. Voxman

# Largo and Allegro
## from Sonata VI

G. F. HANDEL
Transcribed by H. Voxman

**Allegro**

# Élégie

J. Ed. BARAT
Edited by H. Voxman

# Introduction and Rondo

LEROY OSTRANSKY

# Recitative and Allegro

PAUL KOEPKE

Allegro appassionata (♩ = 104)

# Fantaisie Mauresque

F. COMBELLE
Edited by H. Voxman

# Concertante

E. PALADILHE
Transcribed by H. Voxman

Allegro non troppo

60

# First Concertino

GEORGES GUILHAUD
Transcribed by H. Voxman

Allegretto